Contents

No More Bubblegum

WHO COULD have envisioned Occupy Wall Street and its sudden wildflower-like profusion in cities large and small? John Carpenter did. Almost a quarter of a century ago (1988), the master of date-night terror (*Halloween, The Thing*, etc.) wrote and directed *They Live*–depicting the Age of Reagan as a catastrophic alien invasion. It remains his subversive tour de force.

Indeed, who can ever forget the brilliant early scenes of the huge third-world shantytown reflected across the Hollywood Freeway by the sinister mirror-glass of Bunker Hill's corporate skyscrapers? Or Carpenter's portrayal of billionaire bankers and evil mediacrats ruling over a pulverized American working class living in tents on a rubble-strewn hillside and begging for casual jobs?

From this negative equality of homelessness and despair, and thanks to the magic dark glasses found by the enigmatic Nada (played by Roddy Piper), the proletariat finally achieves interracial unity, sees through the subliminal deceptions of capitalism, and gets angry. Very angry.

Yes, I know, I'm reading ahead. The Occupy the World movement is still looking for its magic glasses (program, demands, strategy, and so on) and its anger remains on Gandhian low heat.

But, as Carpenter foresaw, force enough Americans out of their homes and/or careers (or at least torment tens of millions with the possibility) and something new and huge will begin to slouch toward Goldman Sachs. And unlike the Tea Party, so far it has no puppet strings.

One of the most important facts about the current uprising is simply that it has occupied the street and created an existential identification with the homeless.

Quite frankly, my generation, trained in the civil rights movement, would have thought first of sitting in the buildings and waiting for the police to drag and club us out the door. (Today, pepper spray and 'pain compliance techniques are preferred by the cops.)

In 1965, when I was just eighteen and on the national staff of Students for a Democratic Society, I planned a sit-in at the Chase Manhattan Bank, a partner in apartheid for its key role in financing South Africa after the massacre of peaceful demonstrators. It was the first protest on Wall Street in a generation. Forty-one people were hauled away by the NYPD.

I still think that taking over the skyscrapers is a splendid idea, but for a later stage in the struggle. The genius of Occupy Wall Street, for now, is that it has temporarily liberated some of the most expensive real estate in the world and turned a privatized square into a magnetic public space and catalyst for protest.

Our sit-in forty-six years ago was a guerrilla raid; this is Wall Street under siege by the Lilliputians. It's also the triumph of the supposedly archaic principle of face-to-face, dialogic organizing. Social media is important, sure, but not omnipotent. Activist self-organization—the crystallization of political will from free discussion—still thrives best in an actual urban forum.

Put another way, most of our Internet conversations are preaching to the choir; even the mega-sites like MoveOn.com are tuned to the channel of the already converted, or at least their probable demographic.

The occupations likewise are lightning rods, first and above all, for the scorned, alienated ranks of progressive Democrats, but, in addition, they appear to be breaking down generational barriers, providing the missing common ground, for instance, for imperiled middle-age schoolteachers to compare notes with pauperized young college graduates.

More radically, the encampments have become symbolic sites for healing the divisions within the New Deal coalition inflicted during the Nixon years. As Jon Wiener observes in his always smart blog at *The Nation*, "hard hats and hippies—together at last."

Indeed. Who could not be moved when AFL-CIO president Richard Trumka—who brought his coal miners to Wall Street in 1989 during their bitter but ultimately successful strike against Pittston Coal Company—called upon his broad-shouldered women and men to "stand guard" over Zuccotti Park in the face of an expected attack by the NYPD?

ALTHOUGH OLD radicals like me are too apt to declare each new baby the messiah, this child has the rainbow sign. I believe that we're seeing the rebirth of the quality that so markedly defined the ordinary people of my parents' generation (migrants and strikers of the

Great Depression): a broad, spontaneous compassion and solidarity based on a dangerously egalitarian ethic.

Stop and give a hitchhiking family a ride. Never cross a picket line, even when your family can't pay the rent. Share your last cigarette with a stranger. Steal milk when your kids have none and then give half to the little kids next door (this is what my own mother did repeatedly in 1936). Listen carefully to the quiet, profound people who have lost everything but their dignity. Cultivate the generosity of the "we."

What I mean to say, I suppose, is that I'm most impressed by those folks who've rallied to defend the occupations despite often significant differences in age, social class, and race. But equally, I adore the gusty kids who are ready to face the coming winter on freezing streets, just like their homeless sisters and brothers.

But—back to strategy—what's the next link in the chain (in Lenin's sense) that needs to be grasped? How imperative is it for the wildflowers to hold a convention, adopt programmatic demands, and thereby put themselves up for bid on the auction block of the 2012 elections? Obama and the Democrats will certainly, and perhaps desperately, need their energy and authenticity.

But the occupationistas are unlikely to put themselves or their extraordinary self-organizing process up for sale. Personally, I lean toward the anarchist position and its obvious imperatives.

First, expose the pain of the 99 percent. Put Wall Street on trial. Bring Harrisburg, Loredo, Riverside, Camden, Flint, Gallup, and Holly Springs to downtown New York. Confront the predators with their victims. A national tribunal on economic mass murder.

Second, continue to democratize and productively occupy public space (i.e., reclaim the commons). The veteran Bronx activist-historian Mark Naison has proposed a bold plan for converting the derelict and abandoned spaces of New York into survival resources (gardens, campsites, playgrounds) for the unsheltered and unemployed. The Occupy protestors across the country now know what it's like to be homeless and banned from sleeping in parks or under a tent. All the more reason to break the locks and scale the fences that separate unused space from urgent human needs.

Third, keep our eyes on the real prize. The great issue is not raising taxes on the rich or achieving a better regulation of banks. It's economic democracy—the right of ordinary people to make macro-decisions about social investment, interest rates, capital flows, job creation, global warming, and the like. If the debate isn't about economic power, it's irrelevant.

Fourth, the movement must survive the winter in order to fight the power in the next spring. It's cold on the street in January. Bloomberg and every other mayor and local ruler are counting on a hard winter to deplete the protests. Thus it's all-important to reinforce the occupations over the long Christmas break. Put on your overcoat.

Finally, we must calm down—the itinerary of the current protest is totally unpredictable. But if we erect a lightning rod, we shouldn't be surprised if lightning eventually strikes.

Bankers recently interviewed in the *New York Times* seem to find the Occupy protests little more than a nuisance—based, they claim, on an unsophisticated understanding of the financial sector.

They should be more humble. Indeed, they should probably tremble before the image of the tumbril

Four and a half million manufacturing jobs have been lost in the United States since 2000, and an entire generation of college graduates now face the highest downward mobility in American history. Since 1987, African Americans have lost more than half of their net worth; Latinos, an incredible two-thirds.

Wreck the American dream and the common people will put some serious hurt on you. Or as Nada explains to his unwary assailants in Carpenter's great film:

"I have come here to chew bubblegum and kick ass. . . . and I'm all out of bubblegum."

Crash Club

What happens when three sputtering economies collide?

WHEN MY old gang and I were fourteen or fifteen years old, many centuries ago, we yearned for immortality in the fiery wreck of a bitchin' '40 Ford or '57 Chevy. Our J. K. Rowling was Henry Felsen, the ex-Marine who wrote the bestselling masterpieces *Hot Rod* (1950), *Street Rod* (1953), and *Crash Club* (1958).

Officially, his books—highly praised by the National Safety Council—were deterrents, meant to scare my generation straight with huge dollops of teenage gore. In fact, he was our asphalt Homer, exalting doomed teenage heroes and inviting us to emulate their legend.

One of his books ends with an apocalyptic collision at a crossroads that more or less wipes out the entire graduating class of a small Iowa town. We loved this passage so much that we used to read it aloud to each other.

It's hard not to think of the great Felsen, who died in 1995, while browsing the business pages these days. There, after all, are the Tea Party Republicans, accelerator punched to the floor, grinning like demons as they approach Deadman's Curve. (John Boehner and David Brooks, in the back seat, are of course screaming in fear.)

The Felsen analogy seems even stronger when you leave local turf for the global view of things. From the air, where those Iowa cornstalks don't conceal the pattern of blind convergence, the world economic situation looks distinctly like a crash waiting to happen. From three directions, the United States, the European Union, and China are speeding toward the same intersection. The question is: will anyone survive to attend the prom?

Shaking the Three Pillars of McWorld

Let me reprise the obvious but seldom discussed. Even if debt-limit doomsday is averted, Obama has already hocked the farm and sold the kids. With breathtaking contempt for the liberal wing of his own party, he's offered to put the sacrosanct remnant of the New Deal safety net on the auction block to appease a hypothetical "center" and win reelection at any price. (Dick Nixon, old socialist, where are you now that we need you?)

As a result, like the Phoenicians in the Bible, we'll sacrifice our children (and their schoolteachers) to Moloch, now called Deficit. The bloodbath in the public sector, together with an abrupt shutoff of unemployment benefits, will negatively multiply through the demand side of the economy until joblessness is in teenage digits and Lady Gaga is singing "Brother, Can You Spare a Dime?"

Lest we forget, we also live in a globalized economy where Americans are the consumers of last resort and the dollar is still the safe haven for the planet's hoarded surplus value. The new recession that the Republicans are engineering with such impunity will instantly put into doubt all three pillars of McWorld, each already shakier than generally imagined: American consumption, European stability, and Chinese growth.

Across the Atlantic, the European Union is demonstrating that it is exclusively a union of big banks and mega-creditors, grimly determined to make the Greeks sell off the Parthenon and the Irish emigrate to Australia. One doesn't have to be a Keynesian to know that, should this happen, the winds will only blow colder thereafter. (If German jobs have so far been saved, it is only because China and the other BRICs—Brazil, Russia, and India—have been buying so many machine tools and Mercedes-Benzes.)

Boardwalk Empire Times 160

China, of course, now holds up the world, but the question is: for how much longer? Officially, the People's Republic of China is in the midst of an epochal transition from an export-based to a consumer-based economy. The ultimate goal of this is not only to turn the average Chinese into a suburban motorist, but also to break the perverse dependency that ties China's growth to an American trade deficit Beijing must, in turn, finance in order to keep the yuan from appreciating.

Unfortunately for the Chinese, and possibly the world, that country's planned consumer boom is quickly morphing into a dangerous real-estate bubble. China has caught the Dubai virus, and now every city there with more than a million inhabitants (at least 160 at last count) aspires to brand itself with a Rem Koolhaas skyscraper or a destination mega-mall. The result has been an orgy of over-construction.

Despite the reassuring image of omniscient Beijing mandarins in cool control of the financial system, China actually seems to be functioning more like 160 iterations of *Boardwalk Empire*, where big-city political bosses and allied private developers forge their own backdoor deals with giant state banks.

In effect, a shadow banking system has arisen, with big banks moving loans off their balance sheets into phony trust companies and thus evading official caps on total lending. Last week, Moody's Investors Service reported that the Chinese banking system was concealing half a trillion dollars in problematic loans, mainly for municipal vanity projects. Another rating service warned that non-performing loans could constitute as much as 30 percent of bank portfolios.

Real-estate speculation, meanwhile, is vacuuming up domestic savings as urban families, faced with soaring home values, rush to invest in property before they are priced out of the market. (Sound familiar?) According to *Business Week*, residential housing investment now accounts for 9 percent of the gross domestic product, up from only 3.4 percent in 2003.

So, will Chengdu become the next Orlando, or China Construction Bank the next Lehman Brothers? Odd, the credulity of so many otherwise conservative pundits who have bought into the idea that the Chinese Communist leadership has discovered the law of perpetual motion, creating a market economy immune to business cycles or speculative manias.

If China has a hard landing, it will also break the bones of leading suppliers like Brazil, Indonesia, and Australia. Japan, already mired in recession after triple mega-disasters, is acutely sensitive to further shocks from its principal markets. And the Arab Spring may turn to winter if new governments cannot grow employment or contain the inflation of food prices.

As the three great economic blocs accelerate toward synchronized deep recession, I find that I'm no longer as thrilled as I was at fourteen by the prospect of a classic Felsen ending—all tangled metal and young bodies.

A sample passage from Henry Felsen's 1950 novel *Hot Rod*:

The crushed pile of twisted metal that had once been My-Son-Ralph's Chevy was on its back in the ditch, its wheels up like paws of a dead dog. Two of the wheels were smashed, and two were turning slowly. Something that looked like a limp, ripped-open bag of laundry hung halfway out of a rear window. That was Marge.

"*The motor of Ralph's car had been driven back through the frame of the car, and its weight had made a fatal spear of the steering column. Somewhere in the mashed tangle of metal, wood and torn upholstery was Ralph. And deeper yet in the pile of mangled steel, wedged in between jagged sheet steel on one side, and red hot metal on the other, was what had been the shapely black head and dainty face of LaVerne.*

"*Walt's car had spun around after being hit, and had rolled over and along the highway. It had left a trail of shattered glass, metal, and dark, motionless shapes that had been broken open like paper bags before they rolled to a stop. These had been Walt's laughing passengers. Pinned inside his wrecked car, beyond knowing that battery acid ran in his eyes, lay Walt Thomas. Somehow the lower half of his body had been twisted completely around, and hung by a shred of skin.*

Protest
in the Drivers Seat

T HE SICKENING repercussion of hardwood against a protestor's skull is the soundtrack to too much of American history.

If you think being a heavyweight boxer or an NFL wide receiver is an invitation to brain damage, try being an anticapitalist.

Especially when you face an unholy alliance of arrogant bankers, sneering stockbrokers, and liberal Democratic mayors, as in L.A., Portland, Seattle, and Atlanta. Or when your civil liberties exist purely at the sufferance of a billionaire municipal autocrat with Louis XIV tendencies like New York's Michael Bloomberg.

Few events in a young activist's life are as memorably disturbing as the first time you look into a cop's eyes a few anxious inches from your face and find only robotic, murderous hatred staring back at you.

In my day, this dehumanizing fury had usually been programmed somewhere in Vietnam's Central Highlands or the Mekong Delta. Today it was likely implanted in a place called Fallujah or Kandahar.

No doubt it is an important rite of passage to a fuller humanity to become, at least for a few terrifying moments, just another body to be beaten.

But—ouch—I'm not very brave and don't like being clubbed, pummeled, tightly handcuffed, or dragged by my hair (one reason, I suppose, why I've always worn a crew cut).

I prefer to lock myself safely in my car and drive to protests, carefully obeying speed limits and traffic signs. Perhaps humming a crackled version of "American Pie" or singing a few rousing verses from "O Canada."

Indeed, it was Canadian autoworkers, during a brutal Ford strike in fall 1945, who first turned the class struggle into a drive-in.

At the end of World War II, the Ford complex in Windsor, Ontario, was the largest factory in Canada, with about fifteen thousand workers, and Ford management counted on provincial Tories to break the strike with unprecedented police violence.

After days of being harassed by Ontario cops and less-than-heroic Mounties (actually Canada's FBI), the autoworkers borrowed an idea from an earlier UAW protest in Detroit and simply parked two thousand family Fords around the Ford plant.

The Tories' only answer to the great auto blockade was a briefly mulling over a plan to use army tanks to crash through the strikers' cars. An armored regiment was put on alert. Then Ford and its political allies blinked.

Good idea?

Darn right.

Independent owner-operator truckers have used the same tactic on numerous occasions in the last forty years, beginning with the oil price crisis in the 1970s. They've shut down interstates and blockaded city halls, while their sound systems blasted out "Convoy," C. W. McCall's great anthem of eighteen wheel rebellion.

Cause we got a great big convoy rockin' thru the night, yeah, we got a great big convoy, ain't she a beautiful sight?

Come on and join our convoy, ain't nothin' gonna get in our way. We gonna roll this truckin' convoy 'cross the USA.'

No need, of course, to use Fords. As Dinah Shore used to sing, "See the USA in a Chevrolet"—or a Toyota, a VW, a slope-nosed Kenworth "anteater," or, more correctly, your Schwinn retro-city bike. Just keep the convoy rollin'.

Indeed, the next stage of protest could be considered a nostalgic analogy to an old-fashioned family Sunday drive.

Cruise slowly by the Stock Exchange ("look, kids, here's where the dudes who stole our house work") or keep circling and ogling your local police headquarters ("awesome architecture—let's stop and wave").

Or, best of all: "That's Lloyd Bankfein's home. Now whatyathinkofthat? He's president of Goldman Sachs. He got paid fifty-eight million dollars in 2007, so he must really work harder than anyone else on earth. Let's honk the horn and say howdy to good ole Lloyd."

Remember, safety first, so don't drive like that little old lady from Pasadena.

Stay at the exact speed limit, or, better, at the legal minimum. Always set a good example for the two thousand similarly inclined leisure drivers behind you. They may also want to slow down and sightsee.

This is the ultimate American way: protesting in a car (or on a bike) while obeying the law. The possibilities for serene family tourism are endless and mind-boggling.

Wow, perhaps even apocalyptic.

But, out of respect to Bill McKibben and the anti-globa- warming movement, please carpool to shut down Wall Street.

Can Obama See the Grand Canyon?

On presidential blindness and economic catastrophe

LET ME begin, very obliquely, with the Grand Canyon and the paradox of trying to see beyond cultural or historical precedent. The first European to look into the depths of the great gorge was the conquistador Garcia López de Cárdenas in 1540. He was horrified by the sight and quickly retreated from the South Rim. More than three centuries passed before Lieutenant Joseph Christmas Ives of the US Army Corps of Topographical Engineers led the second major expedition to the rim. Like Garcia López, he recorded an "awe that was almost painful to behold." Ives's expedition included a well-known German artist, but his sketch of the Canyon was wildly distorted, almost hysterical. Neither the conquistadors nor the Army engineers, in other words, could make sense of what they saw; they were simply overwhelmed by unexpected revelation. In a fundamental sense, they were blind, because they lacked the concepts necessary to organize a coherent vision of an utterly new landscape.

Accurate portrayal of the Canyon only arrived a generation later when the Colorado River became the obsession of the one-armed Civil War hero John Wesley Powell and his celebrated teams of geologists and artists. They were like Victorian astronauts reconnoitering another planet. It took years of brilliant fieldwork to construct a conceptual framework for taking in the canyon. With "deep time" added as the critical dimension, it was finally possible for raw perception to be transformed into consistent vision. The result of their work, *The Tertiary History of the Grand Canyon District*, published in 1882, is illustrated by

masterpieces of draftsmanship that, as Powell's biographer Wallace Steg-
ner once pointed out, "are more accurate than any photograph." That is
because they reproduce details of stratigraphy usually obscured in cam-
era images. When we visit one of the famous viewpoints today, most of
us are oblivious to how profoundly our eyes have been trained by these
iconic images or how much we have been influenced by the idea, popu-
larized by Powell, of the Canyon as a museum of geological time.

But why am I talking about geology? Because, like the Grand
Canyon's first explorers, we are looking into an unprecedented abyss
of economic and social turmoil that confounds our previous percep-
tions of historical risk. Our vertigo is intensified by our ignorance of
the depth of the crisis or any sense of how far we might ultimately fall.

Weimar Returns in Limbaughland

Let me confess that, as an aging socialist, I suddenly find myself feel-
ing like the Jehovah's Witness who opens his window to see the stars
actually falling out of the sky. Although I've been studying Marxist
crisis theory for decades, I never believed I'd actually live to see financial capitalism commit suicide or hear the International Monetary
Fund warn of imminent "systemic meltdown." Thus, my initial reac-
tion to Wall Street's infamous 777.7 point plunge a few weeks ago
was a very sixties retro elation. "Right on, Karl!" I shouted. "Eat your
derivatives and die, Wall Street swine!" Like the Grand Canyon, the
fall of the banks can be a terrifying but sublime spectacle. But the real
culprits, of course, are not being trundled off to the guillotine; they're
gently floating to earth in golden parachutes. The rest of us may be
trapped on the burning plane without a pilot, but the despicable
Richard Fuld, who used Lehman Brothers to loot pension funds and
retirement accounts, merely sulks on his yacht.

Out in the stucco deserts of Limbaughland, moreover, fear is already
being distilled into a good ol' boy version of the "stab in the back" myth
that rallied the ruined German petit bourgeoisie to the swastika. If you
listen to the rage on commute AM, you'll know that "socialism" has already taken a lien on America, Barack Hussein Obama is terrorism's
Manchurian candidate, the collapse of Wall Street was caused by eld-
erly black people with Fannie Mae loans, and ACORN in its voter reg-
istration drives has long been padding the voting rolls with illegal
brown hordes. In other times, Sarah Palin's imitation of Father Charles
Coughlin—the priest who preached an American Reich in the 1930s
—in drag might be hilarious camp, but with the American way of life
in sudden freefall, the specter of star-spangled fascism doesn't seem

quite so far-fetched. The right may lose the election, but it already possesses a sinister, historically proven blueprint for rapid recovery. Progressives have no time to waste. In the face of a new depression that promises folks from Wasilla to Timbuktu an unknown world of pain, how do we reconstruct our understanding of the globalized economy? To what extent can we look to Obama or any of the Democrats to help us analyze the crisis and then act effectively to resolve it?

Is Obama FDR?

If the Nashville "town hall" debate is any guide, we will soon have another blind president. Neither candidate had the guts or information to answer the simple questions posed by the anxious audience: What will happen to our jobs? How bad will it get? What urgent steps should be taken? Instead, the candidates stuck like flies in flypaper to their obsolete talking points. McCain's only surprise was yet another innovation in deceit: a mortgage relief plan that would reward banks and investors without necessarily saving homeowners. Obama recited his four-point program, infinitely better in principle than his opponent's preferential option for the rich, but abstract and lacking in detail. It remains more a rhetorical promise than the blueprint for the actual machinery of reform. He made only passing reference to the next phase of the crisis: the slump of the real economy and likely mass unemployment on a scale not seen for seventy years.

With baffling courtesy to the Bush administration, he failed to highlight any of the other weak links in the economic system: the dangerous overhang of credit-default swap obligations left over from the fall of Lehman Brothers; the trillion-dollar black hole of consumer credit-card debt that may threaten the solvency of JPMorgan Chase and Bank of America; the implacable decline of General Motors and the American auto industry; the crumbling foundations of municipal and state finance; the massacre of tech equity and venture capital in Silicon Valley; and, most unexpectedly, sudden fissures in the financial solidity of even General Electric. In addition, both Obama and his vice-presidential partner Joe Biden, in their support for Secretary of the Treasury Paulson's plan, avoid any discussion of the inevitable result of cataclysmic restructuring and government bailouts: not "socialism," but ultra-capitalism—one that is likely to concentrate control of credit in a few leviathan banks, controlled in large part by sovereign wealth funds but subsidized by generations of public debt and domestic austerity.

Never have so many ordinary Americans been nailed to a cross of gold (or derivatives), yet Obama is the most mild-mannered William

Jennings Bryan imaginable. Unlike Sarah Palin, who masticates the phrase "the working class" with defiant glee, he hews to a party line that acknowledges only the needs of an amorphous "middle class" living on a largely mythical "Main Street." If we are especially concerned about the fate of the poor or unemployed, we are left to read between the lines, with no help from his talking points which espouse clean coal technology, nuclear power, and a bigger military, but elide the urgency of a renewed war on poverty (as championed by John Edwards in his tragically self-destructed primary campaign). But perhaps inside the cautious candidate is a man whose humane passions transcend his own nearsighted centrist campaign. As a close friend, exasperated by my chronic pessimism, chided me the other day, "Don't be so unfair. FDR didn't have a nuts-and-bolts program either in 1933. Nobody did."

What Franklin D. Roosevelt did possess in that year of bread lines and bank failures, according to my friend, was enormous empathy for the common people and a willingness to experiment with government intervention, even in the face of the monolithic hostility of the wealthy classes. In this view, Obama is MoveOn.org's re-imagining of our thirty-second president: calm, strong, deeply in touch with ordinary needs, and willing to accept the advice of the country's best and brightest.

The Death of Keynesianism

But even if we concede to the Illinois senator a truly Rooseveltian or, even better, Lincolnian strength of character, this hopeful analogy is flawed in at least three principal ways:

First, we can't rely on the Great Depression as analogue to the current crisis, nor upon the New Deal as the template for its solution. Certainly, there is a great deal of déjà vu in the frantic attempts to quiet panic and reassure the public that the worst has passed. Many of Paulson's statements, indeed, could have been directly plagiarized from Herbert Hoover's secretary of the treasury Andrew Mellon, and both presidential campaigns are frantically cribbing heroic rhetoric from the early New Deal. But just as the business press has been insisting for years, this is not the Old American Economy, but an entirely newfangled contraption built from outsourced parts and supercharged by instantaneous world markets in everything from dollars and defaults to hog bellies and disaster futures. We are seeing the consequences of a perverse restructuring that began with the presidency of Ronald Reagan and that has inverted the national income shares of manufacturing (21 percent in 1980; 12 percent in 2005) and those of financial services (15 percent in 1980; 21 percent in 2005). In 1930, the factories may have been shuttered but the

machinery was still intact; it hadn't been auctioned off at five cents on the dollar to China. On the other hand, we shouldn't disparage the miracles of contemporary market technology. Casino capitalism has proven its mettle by transmitting the deadly virus of Wall Street at unprecedented velocity to every financial center on the planet. What took three years at the beginning of the 1930s—that is, the full globalization of the crisis—has taken only three weeks this time around. God help us if, as seems to be happening, unemployment tops the levees at anything like the same speed.

Second, Obama won't inherit Roosevelt's ultimate situational advantage—having emergent tools of state intervention and demand management (later to be called "Keynesianism") empowered by an epochal uprising of industrial workers in the world's most productive factories. If you've been watching the sad parade of economic gurus on *McNeil-Lehrer*, you know that the intellectual shelves in Washington are now almost bare. Neither major party retains more than a few enigmatic shards of policy traditions different from the neoliberal consensus on trade and privatization. Indeed, posturing pseudo-populists aside, it is unclear whether anyone inside the Beltway, including Obama's economic advisors, can think clearly beyond the indoctrinated mindset of Goldman Sachs, the source of the two most prominent treasury secretaries of the last decade.

Keynes, now suddenly mourned, is actually quite dead. More importantly, the New Deal did not arise spontaneously from the goodwill or imagination of the White House. On the contrary, the social contract for the post-1935 Second New Deal was a complex, adaptive response to the greatest working-class movement in our history, in a period when powerful third parties still roamed the political landscape and Marxism exercised extraordinary influence on American intellectual life. Even with the greatest optimism of the will, it is difficult to imagine the American labor movement recovering from defeat as dramatically as it did in 1934–1937. The decisive difference is structural rather than ideological. (Indeed, today's union movement is much more progressive than the decrepit, nativist American Federation of Labor in 1930.) The power of labor within a Walmart-ized service economy is simply more dispersed and difficult to mobilize than in the era of giant urban-industrial concentrations and ubiquitous factory neighborhoods.

Is War the Answer?

The third problem with the New Deal analogy is perhaps the most important. Military Keynesianism is no longer an available *deus ex machina.* Let me explain. In 1933, when FDR was inaugurated, the United States was in full retreat from foreign entanglements, and there was little controversy about bringing a few hundred Marines home from the occupations of Haiti and Nicaragua. It took two years of world war, the defeat of France, and the near-collapse of England to finally win a majority in Congress for rearmament, but when war production finally started up in late 1940 it became a huge engine for the reemployment of the American work force, the real cure for the depressed job markets of the 1930s. Subsequently, American world power and full employment aligned in a way that won the loyalty of several generations of working-class voters.

Today, of course, the situation is radically different. A bigger Pentagon budget no longer creates hundreds of thousands of stable factory jobs, since significant parts of its weapons production are now actually outsourced, and the ideological link between high-wage employment and intervention—good jobs and Old Glory on a foreign shore—while hardly extinct, is structurally weaker than at any time since the early 1940s. Even in the new military (largely a hereditary caste of poor whites, blacks, and Latinos) demoralization is reaching the stage of active discontent and opening up new spaces for alternative ideas.

Although both candidates have endorsed programs including expansion of Army and Marine combat strength, missile defense (a.k.a. "Star Wars"), and an intensified war in Afghanistan that will enlarge the military-industrial complex, none of this will replenish the supply of decent jobs nor prime a broken national pump. However, in the midst of a deep slump, what a huge military budget can do is obliterate the modest but essential reforms that make up Obama's plans for healthcare, alternative energy, and education. In other words, Rooseveltian guns and butter have become a contradiction in terms, which means that the Obama campaign is engineering a catastrophic collision between its national security priorities and its domestic policy goals.

The Fate of Obama-ism

Why don't such smart people see the Grand Canyon? Maybe they do, in which case deception is truly the mother's milk of American politics; or perhaps Obama has become the reluctant prisoner, intellectually as well as politically, of Clintonism: that is to say, of a culturally permissive neoliberalism whose New Deal rhetoric masks the policy spirit of Richard Nixon. It's worth asking, for instance: what in the actual substance of his foreign policy agenda differentiates the Democratic candidate from the radioactive legacy of the Bush Doctrine?

Yes, he would close Guantanamo, talk to the Iranians, and thrill hearts in Europe. He also promises to renew the Global War on Terror (in much the same way that Bush the elder and Clinton sustained the core policies of Reaganism, albeit with a "more human face").

In case anyone has missed the debates, let me remind you that the Democratic candidate has chained himself, come hell or high water, to a global strategy in which "victory" in the Middle East (and Central Asia) remains the chief premise of foreign policy, with the Iraq-style nation-building hubris of Dick Cheney and Paul Wolfowitz repackaged as a "realist" faith in global "stabilization." True, the enormity of the economic crisis may compel President Obama to renege on some of candidate Obama's ringing promises to support an idiotic missile defense system or provocative NATO memberships for Georgia and the Ukraine. Nonetheless, as he emphasizes in almost every speech and in each debate, defeating the Taliban and al-Qaeda, together with a robust defense of Israel, constitutes the keystone of his national security agenda. Under huge pressure from Republicans and blue dog Democrats alike to cut the budget and reduce the exponential increase in the national debt, what choices would President Obama be forced to make early in his administration? More than likely, comprehensive healthcare will be whittled down to a bare-bones plan, "alternative energy" will simply mean the fraud of "clean coal," and anything that remains in the treasury after Wall Street's finished its looting spree will buy bombs to pulverize more Pashtun villages, ensuring yet more generations of embittered mujahideen and jihadis.

Am I unduly cynical? Perhaps, but I lived through the Lyndon Johnson years and watched the War on Poverty, the last true New Deal program, destroyed to pay for slaughter in Vietnam. It is bitterly ironic, but, I suppose, historically predictable that a presidential campaign millions of voters have supported for its promise to end the war in Iraq has now mortgaged itself to a "tougher than McCain" escalation of a hopeless conflict in Afghanistan and the Pakistani tribal frontier. In the best of outcomes, the Democrats will merely trade one brutal, losing war for another. In the worst case, their failed policies may set the stage for the return of Cheney and Rove, or their even-more-sinister avatars.

Field Notes
from the Revolution

Toma el Valle

MY CAR radio reports an Arctic blizzard on Wall Street, but Main Street in El Centro is comfortably baking in 90-degree autumn heat. In California's Imperial Valley, where federally subsidized Colorado River water has irrigated the profits of Anglo *latifundistas* for more than a century and where farmworkers too often die of sunstroke and dehydration on 120-degree days in August, this is fine weather for protest.

Forty or fifty Valley residents are marching down Main, past recently boarded-up storefronts and extinct family businesses, stopping in front of several banks and a McDonald's to chant "No more, no more, no more oppression. The 99 percent is fed up with all the exploitation."

The protest wears two hats—Occupy El Centro and Occupy Imperial County—but both initiatives have now fused into a single emerging network of activists. (Their audacious name in Spanish, which I prefer, is Toma el Valle, or "Take the Valley.")

After some lusty renditions of *El pueblo unido jamas sera vencido* ("Best chant ever," an eighth-grader tells me), the marchers rally under a picnic canopy at Adams Park, where a serape-draped Day of the Dead altar has been erected in memory of the "American Dream."

There are sprays of marigolds, painted papier-mâché skulls, a portrait of a *santo* (Cesar Chavez), corn husks, pumpkin seeds, *pan de muertos*, small American flags, amulets, a plaque with the names of local war dead, and a copy of the 1848 Treaty of Guadalupe Hidalgo. Leaning

on the altar is a large placard: "99%."

But it could also have read "32%"—the official unemployment rate in Imperial County at the beginning of September. According to the Bureau of Labor Statistics, El Centro and its neighboring towns lead the nation's metropolitan areas in joblessness. Likewise, local per capita incomes (about eleven thousand dollars) are today nearly 10 percent less than twenty years ago. Half-finished subdivisions—targeted for sale to extreme long-distance commuters who work in San Diego—are becoming dusty ghost towns, and even the local cemetery is rumored to be in foreclosure.

Statistically, in other words, the *sueño Americano* in the Imperial Valley is almost without a heartbeat. And the outside world is eager to rub salt in the wound.

One yuppie lifestyle site, for example, recently voted El Centro the "worst city" in the United States, while William Vollman, the Forrest Gump of US literary journalism, has depicted Imperial County as the heart of border darkness, if not hell itself, in an immense, sprawling, solipsistic book. His *Imperial* is 1,344 pages long; my edition of Tolstoy's *War and Peace*, 1,296 pages.

After the rally, while organizers are dismantling the altar, I talk to several protesters about outside images of the Valley. One teenager thinks I'm pulling his leg when I describe Vollman's magnum opus: "About El Centro, for real? Why? This is just an ordinary place."

An older Latino man acknowledges the Valley's brutal and extraordinary anti-union past, but also demands respect for its rich cultural core of family life, outdoor recreation, and Mexican heritage. "If our kids leave," he emphasizes, "it's not because they hate the desert, but because there are no decent jobs."

Water Transfer and Death Winds

Later, over apple pie and nachos at a nearby Denny's, I have a chance to interview six of the occupationistas. I'm particularly interested in how they connect the broader themes of greed and inequality to their local situation.

I dub Imperial the most "reactionary" county in California. Susan Massey, a retired schoolteacher from nearby Holtville and a longtime peace activist, is skeptical.

"Poorest, perhaps," she says, but she points to the incremental enfranchisement (80 percent of the population is now Latino) that has ended the long era of overt farm fascism, when shouting anti-plutocratic slogans on Main Street would have resulted in a jail cell or even a lynching.

Electorally, Imperial is now a reliable national Democratic stronghold (represented in Congress by liberal Bob Filner from San Diego), even if voters still overwhelmingly reject gay marriage.

But everyone at the table agrees that the scale of the Valley's unemployment problem far exceeds the meager resources available to local government. And as in southern Louisiana, jobs and the environment are inextricably linked as the region approaches a dangerous tipping point.

Anita Nicklen, a migrant rights advocate and mother of two of the younger protesters, explains the links in a potentially fatal chain. "Farmers are under tremendous pressure to fallow land and sell their water entitlements to San Diego's suburbs. Fewer crops means fewer farm workers and fewer dollars circulating in our local economy. There is also less runoff from irrigation into the rapidly shrinking Salton Sea. Fish die, migratory birds leave, tourists stay home. As the sea dries up, its toxic contents are exposed to the wind."

(A scientist friend of mine later suggests a recipe for making the muck at the bottom of the sea: "Add alkali salts, deadly pesticides, and carcinogenic industrial residues to vast quantities of fertilizer and sewage. Let it dry. Then let it blow. Roll up your car windows and quickly drive as far away as possible.")

Footnote: Desert Chernobyl?

The peril is not theoretical. Los Angeles is currently spending hundreds of millions of dollars to restore parts of Owens Lake, whose water supply was diverted into the LA Aqueduct in 1910, to mitigate the alkali dust storms that for years have created acute respiratory problems in high-desert communities.

But the death of the Salton Sea, an extraordinary reservoir of sinister chemicals, would be like opening Pandora's box, a creeping Chernobyl of respiratory illness and cancer. Partial depopulation of the Imperial and Coachella valleys might follow.

To prevent such an apocalypse, Sacramento has proposed a nine-billion-dollar restoration plan for the sea, but authority for the appropriation has been blocked in court, and the plan must now face the triage of the state debt crisis. Meanwhile, climate change and a long drought in the Colorado Basin have reinforced political pressures to allow much larger water transfers from the Imperial Valley to the coast.

NAFTA Doesn't Trickle Down

I change my line of inquiry. "OK, agriculture will likely decline, but what about the border economy?"

The Imperial Valley stands astride two major NAFTA transport corridors, and its Siamese twin in Mexico, the Mexicali Valley, is rapidly industrializing and diversifying.

El Centro has a population of forty-two thousand; Mexicali, well over a million. Across the border fence is a forest of foreign logos atop bustling maquiladoras: Sanyo, Kenworth, Allied Signal, Goldstar, Nestle, and so on. And an ambitious new industrial park, the "Silicon Border," is fishing in Asia to bring semiconductor manufacturing back to North America.

Surely Mexicali's dynamism must invigorate the Imperial Valley as well?

But no one at Denny's can think of a single new manufacturing plant that free trade has added to the county (there apparently aren't any). On the other hand, everyone has a horror story about the economic and personal impacts of the post-9/11 border.

Anita, who volunteers for Angeles sin Fronteras, a shelter for deported migrants in Mexicali, talks about the cumulative fatigue of purgatorial two-hour-average waits in the northbound lanes to enter California. The delays, she points out, have killed off much of the cross-border retail trade that once nurtured Imperial Valley's malls, markets, and department stores. (Indeed, I discovered a 2007 study by the California Department of Transportation that estimates that the Operation Gatekeeper–like delays have cost Imperial County several thousand jobs and tens of millions of dollars in sales tax receipts.)

The supposed benefits of NAFTA, in other words, haven't trickled down to the Valley. Otherwise, how could you have the nation's highest unemployment rate within spitting distance of one of the continent's busiest trade corridors? And the vigorous interventions by Mexico's state and federal governments to keep Mexicali booming contrasts with the benign neglect of the Imperial Valley's job crisis by both Sacramento and Washington.

Mobilize to Organize

I went to El Centro thinking that I might find a simple meme of the Wall Street protest: a copycat action, unlikely to grow in the hostile climate of Imperial County.

What I discovered, in fact, was a desert flower brought to blossom by a combination of long cultivation (local activist tradition), the existence of a local greenhouse (a physical space for meeting and interaction), and, equally important, lots of sunlight (dialogue via social media).

(I apologize to Occupy El Centro for not being able to interview more of its instigators, as well as for any errors in my interpretation of events.)

First, the importance of having a history:

Some of the older activists—Anita and Susan, for example—are veterans of the 2003 antiwar movement. Although never very large, the Imperial Valley Peace Coalition was a foundation for episodic actions and informal meetings and film viewings. It was also a political nursery where curious teenagers, like Camden Aguilera (now twenty-four) from the town of Imperial took their first steps in dissent.

The peace network recently roared back into existence when Wind Zero, a mysterious San Diego company headed by an ex–Navy SEAL, obtained permission from Imperial County supervisors to build a huge private military-training complex near the desert hamlet of Ocotillo. The plan is almost a carbon copy of Blackwater's notorious attempt several years ago to construct a Goldfinger-like base in the eastern San Diego community of Potrero. Blackwater (now Xe) was eventually defeated in San Diego by a unique grassroots coalition of conservative back-country residents and peace activists; now People Against Wind Zero, supported by Occupy El Centro, is building a similar alliance.

Second, the importance of having a place:

In the current global protests, physical fora and public space have re-established their centrality to rebellion. In the case of the Valley, Camden and Anita both stress the key role of the Center for Religious Science in El Centro, a meditation-focused spiritual center that provides performance space for actors, musicians, and poets and encourages meetings on issues of peace and environmental justice. Camden says the center enables creative countercultures and an alternative realm of ideas to exist in the Valley.

Although activists in the Coachella Valley (a northern extension of the Salton Sink) recently attempted to occupy Palm Desert's Civic Center Park—six were arrested—the Imperial Valley movement is conserving its forces for outreach. As Anita eloquently put it, "We must go from mobilize to organize."

The prime movers of the El Centro demonstration bring together an impressive agenda of 99 percent issues, including migrant rights (Anita), anti–Wind Zero (Susan), feminism (Camden), and veterans' rights (John Hernandez of Brawley).

Occupy El Centro provides a framework both for concentrating forces, as against Wind Zero, and for nurturing new solidarities on both sides of the steel wall that now separates the two Californias.

"Because the Imperial Valley is on the border," Camden said, she looks forward to "opportunities to take part in not only local or national activism, but global activism as well." Anita hopes in particular that they can link with similar groups in Mexicali and begin to build an "Occupy the Border" dimension.

Finally, the virtual community aspect of the Occupy movement enables participation in spite of geographical distance.

Thanks to Facebook, for example, the Valley's college diaspora, including recent UC Santa Cruz graduate Jessica Yocupicio, was able to play an integral role in planning the protest.

According to Susan, "a young man, Sky Ainsworth, ignited the process with an online call for action. When very few people responded, Jessica approached Anita, who she knew from anti–Wind Zero organizing, and she contacted Camden and John Hernandez to start the planning dialogue. Other young people read the blogs and joined in."

At the end of the day, however, occupying El Centro was an exercise in old-fashioned, Jimmy-Higgins-like grit. As Susan explains: "I was moved by the tremendous effort that the young organizers of the rally put forth. None of them have cars and get to work or school by public transportation. In Imperial Valley, buses are so few and far between it means spending two to three hours to go somewhere that is twenty minutes away by car. They are also very dedicated to helping friends and family with problems, so it was amazing that they could bring this off."

The Ten Commandments

(and a Gift from FDR)

A FRIEND IN Canada recently asked me if the protests of the sixties had any important lessons to pass on to the Occupy movement. I told her that one of the few clear memories that I retain from forty-five years ago was a fervent vow never to age into an old fart with lessons to pass on. But she persisted, and the question ultimately aroused my own curiosity. What, indeed, have I learned from my fumbling and bungling lifetime of activism?

Well, unequivocally, I am a pro at coaxing a thousand copies of a flyer from a delicate mimeograph stencil before it disintegrates. (I've promised my kids to take them to the Smithsonian someday to see one of these infernal devices that powered the civil rights and antiwar movements.)

Other than that, I mainly recall injunctions from older or more experienced comrades that I've put to memory as a personal ten commandments.

First, the categorical imperative is to organize—or, rather, to facilitate other people's self-organization. Catalyzing is good, but organizing is better.

Second, leadership must be temporary and subject to recall. The job of a good organizer, as it was often said in the civil rights movement, is to organize herself out of a job, not to become indispensable.

Third, protesters must subvert the media's constant tendency toward metonymy—the designation of the whole by a part, the group by an individual. (Consider how bizarre it is, for instance, that we have "Martin Luther King Day" rather than "Civil Rights Movement Day.") Spokespeople should regularly be rotated and, when necessary, shot.

Fourth, the same warning applies to the relationship between a movement and individuals who participate as an organized bloc. I very much believe in the necessity of an organic revolutionary left, but groups can only claim authenticity if they give priority to building the struggle and keep no secret agenda from other participants.

Fifth, as we learned the hard way in the 1960s, consensus democracy is not identical to participatory democracy. For affinity groups and communes, consensus decision-making may work admirably, but for any large or long-term protest, some form of representative democracy is essential to allow the broadest and most equal participation. The devil, as always, is in the details: ensuring that any delegate can be re-called, formalizing rights of political minorities, guaranteeing affirmative representation, and so on.

I know it's heretical to say so, but good anarchists, who believe in grassroots self-government and concerted action, will find much of value in *Robert's Rules of Order* (simply a useful technology for organized discussion and decision-making).

Sixth, an "organizing strategy" is not only a plan for enlarging participation in protest, but also a concept for aligning protest with the constituencies that bear the brunt of exploitation and oppression.

For example, one of the most brilliant strategic moves of the Black liberation movement in the late 1960s was to take the struggle inside the auto plants in Detroit to form the League of Revolutionary Black Workers.

Today, Occupying the Hood is a similar challenge and opportunity. And the troops occupying the plutocrats' front yard need to respond unequivocally to the human-rights crisis in working-class immigrant communities.

The immigrant rights protests five years ago were among the largest mass demonstrations in US history. Perhaps next May Day we will see a convergence of all movements against inequality on a single day of action.

Seventh, building movements that are genuinely inclusive of unemployed and poor people require infrastructures to provide for basic survival needs like food, shelter, and healthcare. To enable lives of struggle, we must create sharing collectives and redistribute our own resources toward young frontline fighters.

Similarly, we must rebuild the apparatus of movement-committed legal professionals (like the National Lawyers Guild) that played such a vital role in sustaining protest in the face of mass repression in the 1960s.

Eighth, the future of the Occupy movement will be determined less by the numbers in Liberty Park (although its survival is a *sine qua non* of the future) than by the boots on the ground in Dayton, Cheyenne, Omaha, and El Paso. The geographical spread of the protests in many cases equals a diversifying involvement of people of color and trade unionists.

The advent of social media, of course, has created unprecedented opportunities for horizontal dialogue between non-elite activists all over the country and the world. But the Occupy Main Streets still need more support from the better-resourced and mediagenic groups in the major urban and academic centers. A self-financed national speakers' and performers' bureau would be invaluable.

Conversely, it is essential to bring stories from the heartlands and borders to national audiences. The narrative of protest needs to become a mural of what ordinary people are fighting for across the country: stopping strip-mining in Mingo County, West Virginia; reopening hospitals in Laredo; supporting dockworkers in Longview, Washington; fighting a fascist sheriff's department in Tucson; protesting death squads in Tijuana or global warming in Saskatoon; and so on.

Ninth, the increasing participation of unions in Occupy protests—including the dramatic mobilization that forced the NYPD to back down from its attempt to evict OWS—is mutually transformative and raises the hope that the uprising can become a genuine class struggle. Yet at the same time, we should remember that union leaderships, in their majority, remain hopelessly committed to a disastrous marriage with the Democratic Party, as well as to unprincipled inter-union wars that have squandered the promise of a new beginning for labor. Anti-capitalist protesters thus need to more effectively hook up with rank-and-file opposition groups and progressive caucuses within the unions.

Tenth, one of the simplest but most abiding lessons from generations of struggle is the need to speak in the vernacular. The moral urgency of change acquires its greatest grandeur when expressed in shared language.

Indeed, the greatest radical voices—Tom Paine, Sojourner Truth, Frederick Douglas, Eugene Debs, Upton Sinclair, Martin Luther King, Malcolm X, and Mario Savio—have always known how to appeal to Americans in the powerful, familiar words of their major traditions of conscience.

One extraordinary example was Sinclair's nearly successful campaign for governor of California in 1934. His manifesto, *End Poverty in California Now,* was essentially the program of the Socialist Party translated into New Testament parables. It won millions of supporters.

Today, as the Occupy movements debate whether or not they need more concrete political definition, we need to reconsider what demands have the broadest appeals while remaining radical in an anti-systemic sense.

Some young activists might put their Bakunin, Lenin or Slavoj Žižek temporarily aside and dust off a copy of FDR's 1944 campaign platform: the Economic Bill of Rights.

It is a clarion call to social citizenship and a declaration of inalienable rights to employment, housing, healthcare, and a happy life—about as far away from the timid, concessionary Please-Just-Kill-*Half*-the-Jews politics of the Obama administration as might be envisioned.

FDR's fourth-term platform used the language of Jefferson to advance the core demands of the CIO and the social-democratic wing of the New Deal. It was not the maximum program of the Old Left (i.e., democratic social ownership of the banks and large corporations), but it was certainly the most advanced progressive position ever espoused by a major political party or US president.

Today, of course, an Economic Bill of Rights is both an utterly utopian idea and a simple definition of what most Americans existentially need. And the new movements, like the old, must at all cost occupy the terrain of fundamental needs, not of short-term political pragmatism.

In doing so, why not accept the gift of FDR's endorsement?

Conclusion: You Are the Revolution of the Unborn

This pamphlet was compiled at the summit of 2011 (just before Christmas, to be exact), an elevation that gives an encouraging view of the new global landscape of revolt as well as a glimpse of the gathering storms and darkening horizons of 2012 and beyond.

The latter includes the likely collapse of the Eurozone, a "hard landing" for the overheated Chinese economy, and a resultant world depression without an obvious rescue engine or *deus ex machina*. This deepening and increasingly synchronized economic crisis would close most of the doors of reform as well as harden the resistance of bunkered elites like Wall Street bankers, Egyptian generals, and China's state council.

Protest will become even more costly, yet simultaneously more urgent. Class interests and privileges will be ruthlessly clarified by confrontation, but incitements to sectarian hatred and nativism will also grow more hysterical. (Consider the rapid rise and fall of the Israeli social justice movement last summer.)

Monstrous neo-nationalisms with fascist agendas (especially in the aggrieved "creditor" countries of northern Europe) will threaten to sweep away the old, failed parties of neoliberal social democrats and NATO conservatives. Theologies of liberation will contest with theologies of annihilation.

The response from the new protest movements may be feeble, tragic or earth-saving. Never in human history has a young generation, even that of the 1930s and 40s, faced such implacable challenges or carried so much of the weight of the future.

To the extent that global capitalism is incapable of creating future jobs, guaranteeing elemental food security, or adapting civilization to survival in a new and more extreme climate, the very foundations of our unequal and unsustainable societies must be radically changed, quickly and despite barbarous opposition.

The struggles of the next few years will test the possibility of inventing this utopian but necessary new world. Three billion new human beings wait to be born in the lifetimes of those now occupying Wall Street and Tahrir Square. We must become their fierce mothers. This we can clearly see—if not much else—from the small hill on which we stand.

About Haymarket Books

HAYMARKET BOOKS is a nonprofit, progressive book distributor and publisher, a project of the Center for Economic Research and Social Change. We believe that activists need to take ideas, history, and politics into the many struggles for social justice today. Learning the lessons of past victories, as well as defeats, can arm a new generation of fighters for a better world. As Karl Marx said, "The philosophers have merely interpreted the world; the point, however, is to change it."

We take inspiration and courage from our namesakes, the Haymarket Martyrs, who gave their lives fighting for a better world. Their 1886 struggle for the eight-hour day reminds workers around the world that ordinary people can organize and struggle for their own liberation.

For more information and to shop our complete catalog of titles, visit us online at www.haymarketbooks.org.